THOMAS CRANE PUBLIC LIBRARY
QUINCY MASS
CITY APPROPRIATION

FUTURE TRANSPORT
BY AIR

By Steve Parker
Illustrations by David West

 **Marshall Cavendish**
Benchmark

New York

Other Marshall Cavendish Offices:
Marshall Cavendish International (Asia) Private Limited, 1 New Industrial Road, Singapore 536196 • Marshall Cavendish International (Thailand) Co Ltd. 253 Asoke, 12th Flr, Sukhumvit 21 Road, Klongtoey Nua, Wattana, Bangkok 10110, Thailand • Marshall Cavendish (Malaysia) Sdn Bhd, Times Subang, Lot 46, Subang Hi-Tech Industrial Park, Batu Tiga, 40000 Shah Alam, Selangor Darul Ehsan, Malaysia

Marshall Cavendish is a trademark of Times Publishing Limited

Library of Congress Cataloging-in-Publication Data

Parker, Steve, 1952-
By air / Steve Parker.
p. cm. -- (Future transport)
Includes bibliographical references and index.
Summary: "Gives a concise history of travel by land, water, air, or in space, showing the technology available today, in the near future, and in centuries to come"--Provided by publisher.
ISBN 978-1-60870-777-5
1. Aeronautics--Juvenile literature. 2. Air travel--Juvenile literature.
I. Title.
TL547.P2695 2012
387.7--dc22

2011000998

Produced by
David West ☆☆ Children's Books
7 Princeton Court
55 Felsham Road
London SW15 1AZ

Designer: Gary Jeffrey
Illustrator: David West

The photographs in this book are used by permission and through the courtesy of:
Abbreviations: t-top, m-middle, b-bottom, r-right, l-left, c-center.
7 tl, Joost J. Bakker IJmuiden; 7tr, 26br, NASA; 7b, Vincent FOLLIARD; 8b, Design Q; 9m, 30rt, NASA/Boeing, 9b, Yasuhiko Obara Yasobara; 10t, thefixer, 10m, photo by Ted Goldstein, 10m, Piper Aircraft Inc., 10b, RadekS; 11t, iconaircraft.com, 11m, Ciar, 11bl, ELECTRAVIA; 12t, IgarashiDesign, 12m, Daniel Kocyba/Sebastian Schäfer/iStock, 12b, © Eurocopter/Patrick PENNA; 13t, AVX Aircraft Company, 13m, American Dynamics Flight Systems, 13bl, Piasecki Aircraft Corp; 13br, © Garrow Aircraft LLC; 14t, U.S. Navy photo by Ensign John Gay; 14m, NASA, Lockheed Martin Co., 14b, BAE Systems; 15t, Aerion Corp., 15tr, Airbus S.A.S, 15m, 24r, 25br, NASA Dryden, 15b, Reaction Engines LTD; 16b, Stefan Richter; 17t, Gemo-netz; 17m, Schellhaas; 18t, the_tahoe_guy, 18m, Studio Massaud with the scientific partnership of the ONERA, 18b, 25tm, Lockheed Martin; 19t, 23-24, 24b, Northrop Grumman, 19b, worldwide Aeros Corp.; 20t, YVES ROSSY PRESS SERVICE; 20l, jurvetson, 20m, NASA 20b, Martin Jetpack; 21t, U.S Army; 22r, Dave Sizer, 22l, GE Aviation; 23t, EADS, 23m, www.solarimpulse.com, 23br, Burkhard Domke, 23b, Easyjet, 23br, rolls royce plc; 24t, 25tr, United States Air Force; 25m, United States Navy photo by Mass Communication Specialist 3rd Class Kenneth G. Takada; 26, bl, Alessandro Silva/Força Aérea Brasileira, 27bl, CAE; 28t, Lakshmix; 29b, MIT/Aurora Flight Sciences; 30m, Reindy Allendra

Printed in China
135642

Contents

INTRODUCTION

"Here is the news. Due to a computer error this morning, jetcars on the city's northern skyway faced a three-hour delay. Also two people are in the hospital after their hoverbike's anti-gravity drive failed. But on the bright side, the city's climate control is fixed, so the rest of the day will be warm and sunny. Fly safely!"

One day we may travel almost everywhere by air. There could be many kinds of travel craft, from personal jetpacks to airborne buses and floating freightliners.

Science and technology will leap ahead, with inventions we can hardly imagine today. But new technology is only part of the story. How will we make air transport safe and organized? What about fuel use, pollution, and the environment? There are many challenges to conquer before we achieve ultimate freedom and fly like the birds.

FLYING HIGH

Compared to travel by land and sea, air transport has only just started. Powered flight is hardly more than a century old. Since then we have developed all kinds of aircraft, from small family planes to giant jumbo jets carrying over 800 people.

The Wright Flyer III *carried the first air passenger, the Wright's mechanic, Charlie Furnas, in 1908.*

In 1945 the Lockheed Constellation was the first airliner with a pressurized cabin for comfort.

German airship Hindenburg *exploded in a fireball at Lakehurst, New Jersey, in 1937, ending the era of airship travel.*

From 1976 Concorde flew the only regular supersonic (faster-than-sound) passenger services. But after a terrible crash in 2000, the remaining nine Concordes in service retired in 2003.

PLANES TAKE OFF

Brothers Wilbur and Orville Wright flew the first true airplane, their *Wright Flyer*, on December 17, 1903. But plane transport was slow to develop until World War I (1914–1918) brought battles for air power. Then regular mail, passenger, and freight trips began. By the 1930s business was booming.

Flying Wings

Often called the "Flying Wing," the Blended Wing Body design, BWB, looks futuristic but has been tried many times. An early BWB was Germany's Junkers G.38, first flown in 1929. Two were built for regular service, seating over thirty people – six in each wing! The Boeing X-48 model remote-control plane is the latest BWB test design.

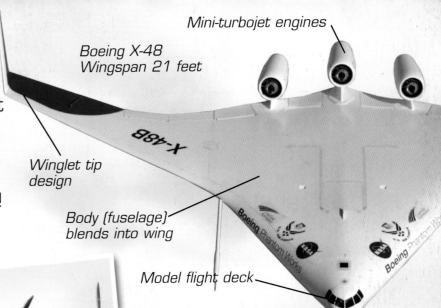

Mini-turbojet engines

Boeing X-48
Wingspan 21 feet

Winglet tip design

Body (fuselage) blends into wing

Model flight deck

Junkers G.38

Taking Shape

Today's basic plane shape dates to the 1930s: a fuselage, two main wings, tailplane (rear wings), and tail fin. Power came from propeller piston engines. Jets first flew in World War II (1939–1945), then jet airliners, like de Havilland Comets and Boeing 707s, in the 1950s. The overall design has changed little. What's the next big step?

"Seemed like a good idea…"

The Vought V-173 "Flying Pancake" of 1942 began a series of disk-shaped aircraft designed for very short take-off and landing, with a possible future as flying cars. But tests were not convincing and the idea soon faded.

The biggest passenger transport is the giant Airbus A380, which first flew in 2005. Its main advance is a "double deck" design with two full-length cabins for passengers.

AIRFRANCE

FUTURE AIRLINERS

Boeing's idea for the Kermit Kruiser (left) *has a large rear wing for less air resistance or drag. The joined wing concept (below) uses a diamond wing design.*

The airline business is tough. Companies fight for customers with the latest planes and schedules. Some people want to get there fast, others like luxury or an energy-efficient aircraft with low pollution. Future airliners may offer all these features.

PLANE SAILING

One way to improve efficiency is to alter the shape of the wings, such as making them long and narrow, like a glider. This can increase the wing's lifting force so the plane "sails" through the air with less engine power, like long-winged soaring seabirds such as the albatross.

"Seemed like a good idea..."

In the 1960s the Aviation Traders Carvair tried to compete with car ferry ships. It flew up to five cars and twenty passengers in less than half the time of a ferry service. But of the twenty-one Carvairs built, eight crashed, and also tickets were hugely costly.

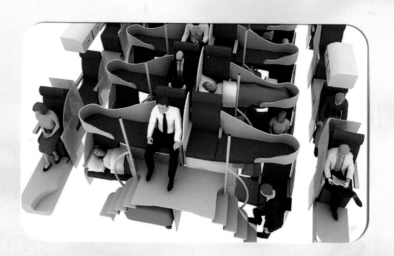

Airliners can change interior layout from one day to the next, with close-packed seats for short trips, then comfortable beds for longer journeys.

Cargo module

Module mover

Passenger module

Loading and unloading freight or passengers takes time and so costs money. In a modular airliner, already-loaded fuselage sections or modules could be quickly moved into position. Total turnaround time on the ground would be more than halved.

The XC-120 Pack Plane from 1950 had a removable cargo pod, similar to containers on road trucks.

Eco Flyers

We have eco-friendly electric cars and electric trains, so why not electric planes? Today's batteries are too heavy and bulky to get off the ground. One possibility is a hybrid with a gas turbine, as used in helicopters. Either the turbines or battery-powered electric motors turn the propellers, while the turbines generate in-flight electricity for recharging.

NASA-Boeing's Sugar Volt concept may fly in 2035. This hybrid will have improved lightweight batteries, electric motors, and turbine engines

Boeing's long-range 787 Dreamliner makes great use of light, strong composite materials to save fuel. It first flew in 2009.

9

LIGHT PLANES

Somewhere between the personal jetpack and the airliner is the light plane of the future. It will carry a family with suitcases on annual vacation—or take a group of friends into the big city for some shopping and a night out.

The fastest of small aircraft are the X-Racer rocket planes of the Rocket Racing League, founded in 2005. Like aerial racing cars they blast along at 300-plus mph (500 km/h).

The Terrafugia Transition folds up for the average garage. On the road the piston engine drives the rear wheel for a speed of 65 mph (100 km/h). In the air it spins the pusher propeller to cruise at 107 mph (172 km/h).

COMBI FLY-DRIVES

Some future light craft will be purpose-designed for flying only. Others may be combinations of car and plane, boat and plane, or even all three. They will take off and land in just a few yards and seconds. They must be stable in the air and simple to control, too, if the driver becomes the pilot.

Piperjet's Altaire (below) is a one-engined VLJ (Very Light Jet) needing just one pilot, with room for up to seven passengers.

Almost an airborne version of the motorcycle, the Samba combined light plane and microlight may be a glimpse of the future.

Icon A5 Amphibious Sportsplane

An alternative to the landing strip is a nearby lake or river—and this is where the Icon A5 comes in. A two-person microlight with a piston-engined pusher-propeller, it can land on water or a prepared ground strip.

The first Icon A5 made its test flight in 2008. If it is licensed for production it should sell for around $150,000.

ICON A5

Wings fold for easy stowage

Rotax 912 microlight engine

Stabilizing skid

Hull-shaped body

"Seemed like a good idea…"

N100D

U.S. aero engineer Moulton Taylor built several Aerocars in the 1940s–1950s, with folding wings and a detachable pusher propeller. Top speed was 60 mph (97 km/h) on the ground and 110 mph (177 km/h) in the air. It had few buyers.

Next Big Step?

The Blended Wing Body or "flying wing" (see page 7) may be the next great advance in light planes. The large wing area does not allow great speed, but it offers plenty of lifting force for low fuel use and quiet flying—much better than a helicopter. One problem is stability, since some BWBs are easily blown around by strong winds.

Electravia's proposed ElectroClub microlight (left), with its near-silent electric motor, looks similar to the Northrop N-9M of the 1940s (right). The N-9M was a one-third scale model to test long-range bomber design.

11

WHIRLYBIRDS

Surely everyone should have a helicopter in the backyard? They are so convenient and useful! But they are also expensive to buy, costly to maintain, and tricky to fly.

Igarashi Design's SNOC single-seater idea is a hybrid of helicopter and motorcycle, powered like most copters by a gas turbine engine.

HOVER FLIES

Copters are naturally unstable, so they need plenty of skilled control or they suddenly tumble out of the sky. Their complex rotor mechanism demands careful adjustment and maintenance, and they are super-thirsty on fuel. Could copters of the future overcome these problems?

Kocyba's Hummel (above) is a planned tandem-rotor, two-seat helicopter that folds up tight. It could be useful as an air taxi to beat traffic jams.

Eurocopter X3's two turbine engines spin both the main rotor and two propellers to boost forward motion. It should fast-cruise at 250-plus mph (400 km/h).

AVX TX Hover Transport

AVX's planned TX converts from a utility road vehicle to a helicopter-like flier in just one minute. Ducted fans push it along in flight and on the ground. In car mode the lift rotors disconnect from the engine and fold back.

Contra-rotating lift rotors

Tires for road driving

Ducted fan propulsion

The proposed American Dynamics AD-150 is a robot ducted-fan plane with fan-shaped wingtip rotors inside collarlike ducts. These point upward for vertical take-off and landing, and swivel forward for normal flight.

Rotor Solutions

As a helicopter's main rotor blades spin one way, its body tries to turn the other way. This is why most copters have a smaller rotor at the back. One answer is the tandem design with two small rotors side by side. Another is contra-rotation with two rotors, one above the other but spinning different ways.

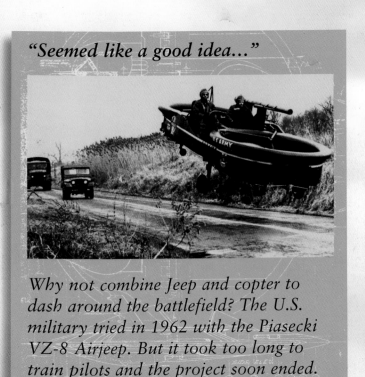

"Seemed like a good idea..."

Why not combine Jeep and copter to dash around the battlefield? The U.S. military tried in 1962 with the Piasecki VZ-8 Airjeep. But it took too long to train pilots and the project soon ended.

The Garrow Verticopter concept has twin tilting fans in the fuselage, which direct air down for take-off and then angle back for normal flight.

13

Quick Jets

In 1947 U.S. test pilot Chuck Yeager broke the "sound barrier" in his Bell X-1 rocket plane. Going supersonic—faster than sound—has been the great test for many aircraft. It looks like an even bigger challenge in the future.

An F-15 Eagle creates a shock wave and sonic boom as it breaks the sound barrier.

A supersonic airliner idea from Lockheed Martin has engines on top of the wings and an upside-down V tailplane. This should quiet the "sonic boom" when going faster than sound, which disturbs people below.

Super-Streamlined

Supersonic planes need an extra-streamlined shape, long and slim, with a pointed nose and tapering tail. This is because pushing through the air creates resistance or drag. At faster-than-sound speed, more than 660 mph (1,000 km/h) at 20,000 feet (6,000 m), normal plane design causes huge drag and gives a very uncomfortable ride.

The BAE Taranis is an experimental combat UAV – unmanned aerial vehicle or robot fighter plane. Its stealth design avoids radar detection. A future version may be able to travel at almost twice the speed of sound.

The Airbus Concept Plane (below) with its weird tail may be the shape of passenger jet travel in 2030.

The ultra-rich like to be one step ahead. Their ultimate will be the SBJ, Supersonic Business Jet, like this proposal from Aerion (above). You could fly from New York to London, have a meeting, and return in one day!

"Seemed like a good idea..."

The Douglas X-3 Stiletto took off in 1952, with the aim of testing long flights at well over supersonic speed. Its pointed shape looked fast, but its engines were too weak, and it could only go supersonic in a steep dive.

Sonic Cruisers

The only supersonic passenger craft was Concorde, from 1976 to 2003. People loved its graceful shape, but it was noisy, thirsty, and not up to modern safety standards. The way is clear for new, safe, quiet, efficient supersonic transports. Zoom!

Large tailplane and tail fin

Turbofan engines

Wide body

Rounded nose

Minimal tail

Long, wide swept wings

Supersonic Aircraft Design

A supersonic cruiser needs a slim fuselage with small stabilizing and control surfaces at each end, in the form of canard wings and a mini-fin. Windows bring construction and heat problems and might be absent.

Delta main wings

Liquid cooled turbojet engines

Canard front wings

Tapered, narrow fuselage

Needle-sharp nose

GROUND EFFECT

Flying high in the sky gives a great view, but keeping up a big plane uses lots of energy and fuel. Maybe the future is with GEVs (Ground-Effect Vehicles) or WIGs (Wing-In-Grounds). They skim just above the water—or the land!

Various GEVs or "ekranoplans" were tested in secret by Russia from the 1950s. Called "Caspian Sea Monsters" the largest weighed over 550 tons— 100 tons more than a fully-loaded Boeing 747 jumbo jet. Rumors say that new versions are now being tested.

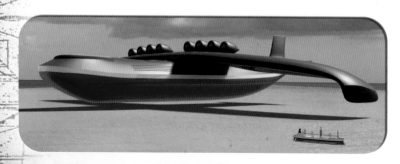

GEVs will probably be too big and heavy to land on normal runways. The fuselage would be shaped like a boat hull for landing and take-off on water, like the old Flying Boat aircraft of the 1930s.

SEA SKIMMERS

In one way, the GEV is halfway to being a hovercraft. It flies so low, just a few yards above the surface, that down-flowing air from under the wings pushes against the surface for cushion-like lift. This gives great savings in the energy needed to keep the craft airborne, so it can carry bigger loads with smaller engines and less fuel. The problem comes when high winds and storms whip up big waves.

The Aquaglide 5 is a small GEV or "light ekranoplan." It can carry five people at a flight speed of 105 mph (170 km/h) or a water speed of 55 mph (88 km/h).

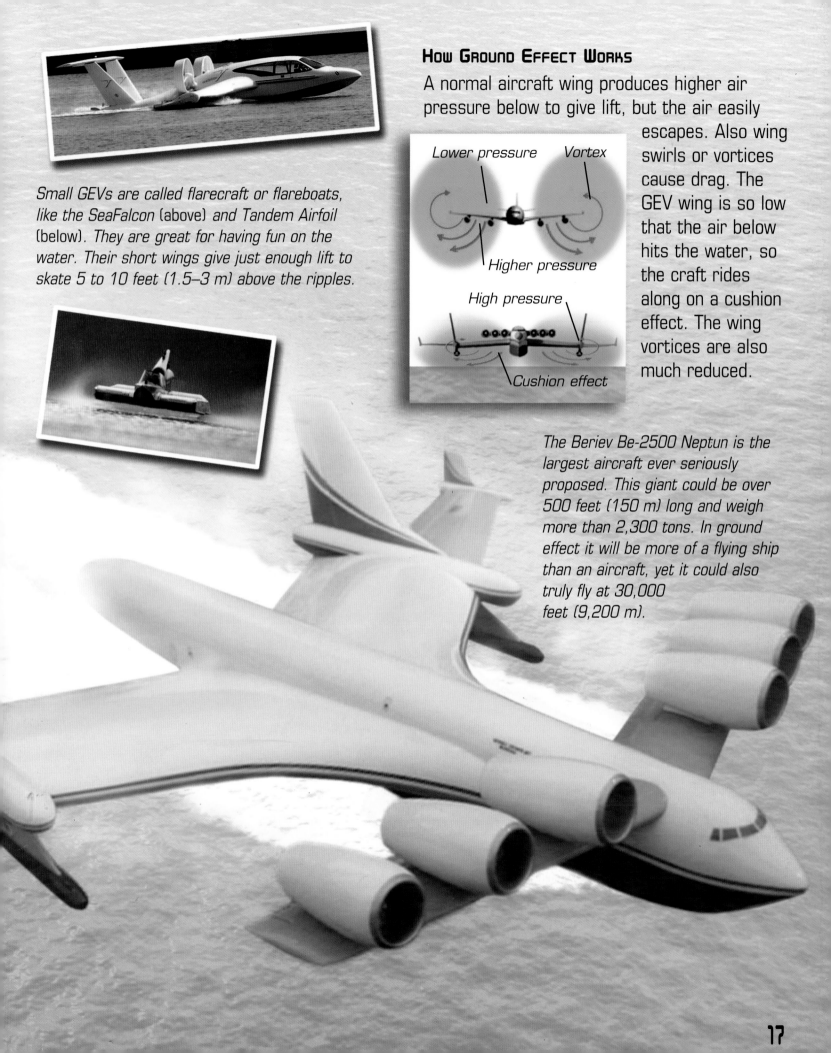

Small GEVs are called flarecraft or flareboats, like the SeaFalcon (above) and Tandem Airfoil (below). They are great for having fun on the water. Their short wings give just enough lift to skate 5 to 10 feet (1.5–3 m) above the ripples.

How Ground Effect Works

A normal aircraft wing produces higher air pressure below to give lift, but the air easily escapes. Also wing swirls or vortices cause drag. The GEV wing is so low that the air below hits the water, so the craft rides along on a cushion effect. The wing vortices are also much reduced.

Lower pressure   Vortex

Higher pressure

High pressure

Cushion effect

The Beriev Be-2500 Neptun is the largest aircraft ever seriously proposed. This giant could be over 500 feet (150 m) long and weigh more than 2,300 tons. In ground effect it will be more of a flying ship than an aircraft, yet it could also truly fly at 30,000 feet (9,200 m).

During the 1930s the "Queens of the Skies" flew thousands of people in enormous luxury. But several fires, explosions, and bad-weather disasters ended the airship's rule. Can new technology help them return?

Modern airships like the AV ZNT are used for tourist flights, sightseeing, and aerial mapping, photography, and filming.

"Seemed like a good idea..."

Aerial Landing Field

This 1934 proposal for a floating airship-airfield had a landing strip for planes to refuel in mid ocean. Newly invented solar panels provided electricity for the electric motor propellers to keep the craft in position.

The Manned Cloud airship could be a flying hotel that circles the world in a few days. At 18,000 feet (5,500 m), forty passengers would enjoy the views.

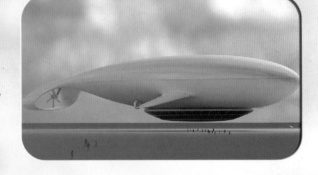

Good and Bad

Unlike winged aircraft, an airship's lift is basically free because it contains lighter-than-air gases, usually helium. It only needs to power forward flight. But this flight may be against the wind, which is where difficulties begin. Rough weather means these giant "gas-bags" have to hide in hangars.

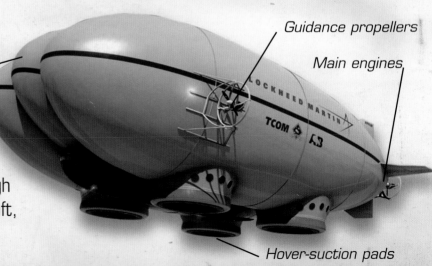

Guidance propellers

Main engines

Triple hull

Hover-suction pads

Lockheed Martin P-791

A possible heavy-load carrier, the triple-bodied P-791 first flew in 2006. It gains the final one-fifth of its lift, just enough to take off, by moving forward like an aircraft, then cruises faster than a normal airship.

The Long Endurance Multi-Intelligence Vehicle (LEMV) is an unmanned "spy airship" being tested by the U.S. military. At 250 feet (76 m) long, it could float-and-fly to 20,000 feet (6,000 m) and stay there for up to three weeks, taking photographs and maneuvering with its six turbo-diesel prop-thrusters.

CARGO BUSTERS

Passengers dislike bad weather delays. But airships could carry huge loads of non-urgent freight to remote areas even without airfields. However, a challenge is how to balance the craft as it picks up or drops off heavy cargo. Powerful computerized pumps could move the gases inside to keep the ship stable.

Planned Aeroscraft hybrids could use a combination of lighter-than-air gases, wings, and similar aerodynamic shapes for extra lift and control. Thrust comes from propellers spun by electric motors powered by solar cells covering the upper body.

PERSONAL FLIGHT

Most people dream of strapping on a backpack and zooming off into the sky. Personal flight may be the ultimate, but if things go wrong, you can only blame the pilot!

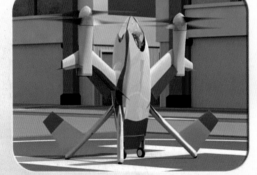

In 2008 Yves Rossy crossed the English Channel with his rocket-wing. He has had several near-misses and some hard landings, too.

Many kinds of jetpacks, like this Rocket belt, have been tested over the years. But a wrong twitch of the controls can lead to disaster.

NASA's electric Puffin idea takes off like a helicopter, then flattens out for normal flight. Almost silent, it could be ideal for military spies.

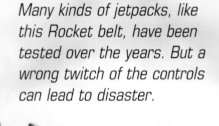

FLYING SOLO

There are several ways of powering one-person flight. They include small helicopter rotors or ducted fans, mini-jets, baby rockets, and blasts of compressed gas. With powerful machinery at the pilot's back or side, danger is truly just around the corner. But the feeling of freedom could be worth the risk.

MARTIN JETPACK

Not actually powered by a jet engine, the Martin Jetpack (right) works by "jets" of air from two ducted fans driven by a lightweight piston engine. After test flights in 2008, its controls are now being improved.

Martin Jetpack demonstration

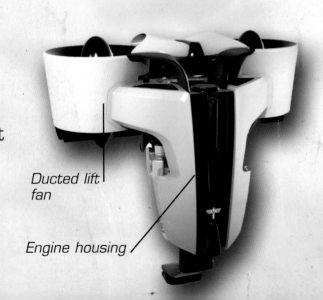

Ducted lift fan

Engine housing

PERSONAL SPACE INVADERS

Jetpack flying needs huge care. It is difficult to see what's behind—or above, below, even to the sides. Future technology could bring a screen or heads-up display to show all objects around and automatically steer away to avoid bumps or serious crashes.

Boots, backpacks, pods, and wings might be used for different kinds of flying trips.

"*Seemed like a good idea...*"

The 1955 Flying Platform aimed to give military scouts an aerial battlefield view, hover, and beat a quick retreat. But the scout stood just above whirling rotor blades—amazingly dangerous!

21

AERO POWER

Most air transport relies on jets, piston-engined props, and the occasional rocket. Will a new kind of motor or power plant take over in years to come?

PulseJet Racer's engines will have no moving parts. They suck in a "blob" of air, burn it, send the gas blast rearward, then do the same again, for almost continuous pulses of thrust.

The GEnx turbofan jet (left) powers the Boeing Dreamliner (above). The huge bypass fan, more than 9 feet (2.7 m) across, provides nine-tenths of the total thrust, and the jet exhaust does the rest.

"Seemed like a good idea..."

REVOLUTION IN THE AIR

Early jet engines relied on the blast of superhot exhaust gases for thrust. Modern turbofans get most propulsion from the enormous fanlike turbine at the front that works like a propeller. Future jets could have new mechanisms such as oarlike paddles or flapping mini-wings.

Steam powered the early cars, and also a few early aircraft, especially in the 1930s. But the fuel, usually coal or coke, was too heavy and difficult to feed smoothly into the boiler.

First flying in 2010, this Cri-Cri ultralight's piston engines have been replaced by four electric motors driven by lithium-polymer batteries.

Airborne Alternatives

If future batteries weigh less and last longer, then the electric plane could be the next big step. Another hope is more efficient solar panels on the wings, to turn enough sunlight into electricity for the flight motors even when it's cloudy. But night flights would still need battery power!

Solar Impulse has huge wings over 200 feet (61 m) across, yet carries just one person. The wings are covered with solar cells to charge the batteries for the four prop-spinning motors.

Propfans

Also called open rotors, these jets have fanlike rotor blades on the outside, usually at the rear. They use up to one-third less fuel than other jets, but they are slow and noisy. Future designs could solve these problems.

Exhaust gases

Open rotor blades

Air intake

The propfan's engine core is similar to a normal jet engine (left), with the addition of fans or rotors on the outside. Propfans could be used for budget short-distance transport (right).

Engine core

23

MILITARY AIRCRAFT

Air power is not just about speed, guns, and bombs. Future warplanes will be ultra-aerobatic, super-smart, and have the latest stealth features before the enemy knows about them.

The F-117 Nighthawk was the first true stealth plane.

SHHHH! STEALTH

"Stealth" means sneaking into action without the enemy knowing. The plane's shape and surface scatters radar waves to keep it off radar screens. Hot engine exhaust gases are cooled and spread so infra-red sensors cannot detect them. Noise is reduced, too, and radio communications are kept to a minimum in case of eavesdropping.

"Seemed like a good idea..."

The Ryan X-13 Vertijet of 1955 took off and landed vertically, the seat tilting as the pilot levelled out. Luckily plans to launch it from a tube inside a submarine were scrapped.

Due to test-fly in 2020, the Switchblade robot spyplane has no fuselage or tail, just two jet engines under a wing 200 feet (61 m) long. In slow flight the wing is at right angles to the engines. At high speed it swivels to point forward at a 60° angle.

24

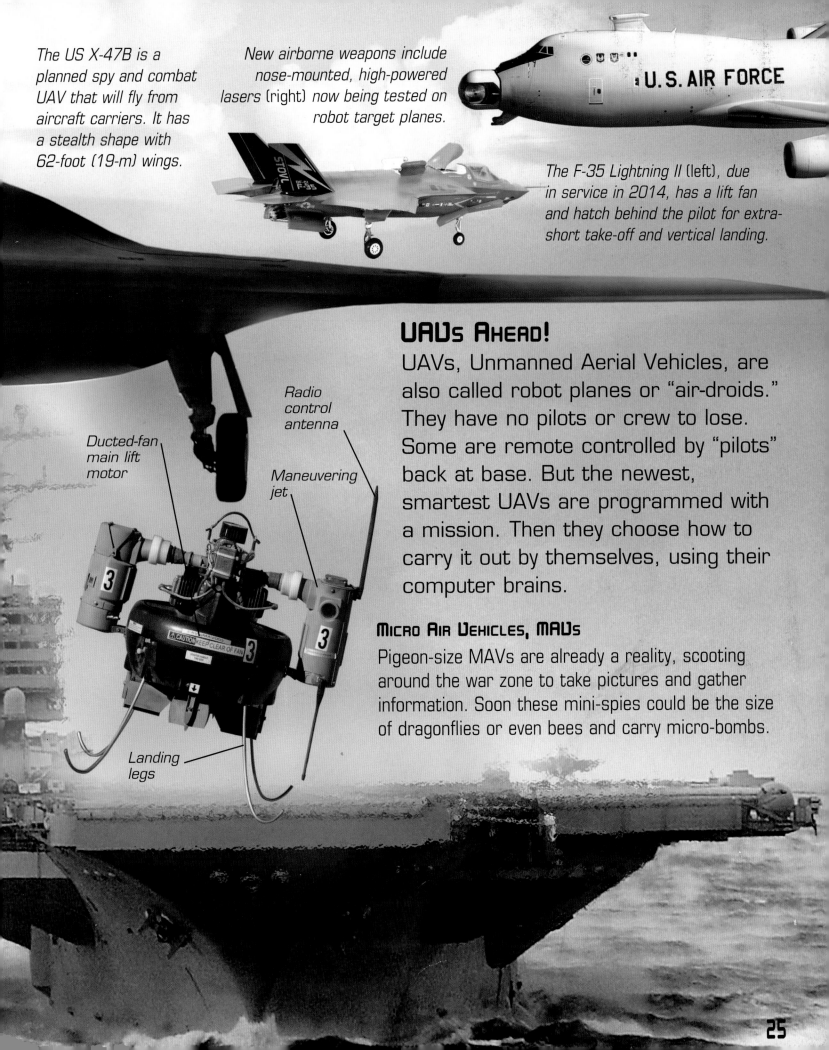

The US X-47B is a planned spy and combat UAV that will fly from aircraft carriers. It has a stealth shape with 62-foot (19-m) wings.

New airborne weapons include nose-mounted, high-powered lasers (right) now being tested on robot target planes.

U.S. AIR FORCE

The F-35 Lightning II (left), due in service in 2014, has a lift fan and hatch behind the pilot for extra-short take-off and vertical landing.

Radio control antenna

Ducted-fan main lift motor

Maneuvering jet

Landing legs

UAVs Ahead!

UAVs, Unmanned Aerial Vehicles, are also called robot planes or "air-droids." They have no pilots or crew to lose. Some are remote controlled by "pilots" back at base. But the newest, smartest UAVs are programmed with a mission. Then they choose how to carry it out by themselves, using their computer brains.

Micro Air Vehicles, MAVs

Pigeon-size MAVs are already a reality, scooting around the war zone to take pictures and gather information. Soon these mini-spies could be the size of dragonflies or even bees and carry micro-bombs.

AIR SAFETY

Air transport is not only the fastest way to travel, it's also one of the safest. New technology will reduce risks even more, as aircraft get smarter and airports become more secure.

IN THE AIR

Sadly, accidents can happen. The key is to lessen the risks at every stage. Aircraft have main systems such as electrics, hydraulics, and navigation. Then there are secondary or back-up systems in case the main ones fail. The newest designs often have tertiary systems that back up the back-ups.

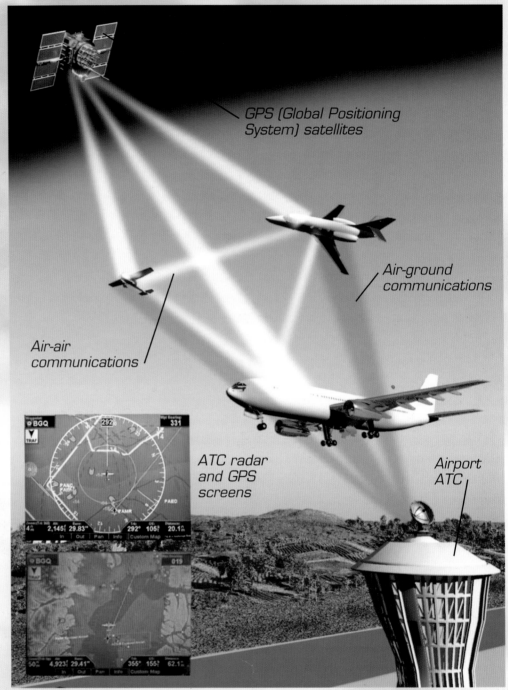

GPS (Global Positioning System) satellites

Air-ground communications

Air-air communications

ATC radar and GPS screens

Airport ATC

"Black box" flight recorders are usually orange, to be found by searchers. They record voices and many aircraft instruments.

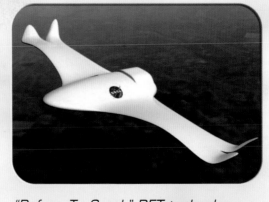

"Refuse To Crash" RFT technology may mean aircraft change or morph their shape, such as wings thickening to cope with stormy weather.

Next-generation navigation includes Automatic Dependent Surveillance-Broadcast, ADS-B. Each aircraft regularly works out its position and heading using satellites (GPS or satnav) and broadcasts this for receivers nearby, including other aircraft and ATC, Air Traffic Control.

Future Attribute Screening Technology (FAST)

FAST cameras and sensors will check passengers closely for body movements and temperature, facial expressions, flushing, nervous twitches, breathing, wide pupils, and other suspicious signs.

Infra-red sensors for temperature

Full body scanner

CCTV motion analyzer

Observer station

Retinal scanner

As passengers pass through security checks, FAST builds up a complete picture of their behavior. It alerts staff to anything unusual before a suspect reaches the plane.

Pilots spend many hours each year in ground-based flight simulators. They learn how to react to a huge range of problems from thick fog to an engine fire.

Design and Training

Every air accident is analyzed carefully for what went wrong and why, to learn lessons for the future. This allows plane designers to use better shapes and improved materials. Pilots will train harder than ever and have regular tests and checks. With all this effort, safety can only improve.

BOEING 787
CAE
CAE 7000 Series

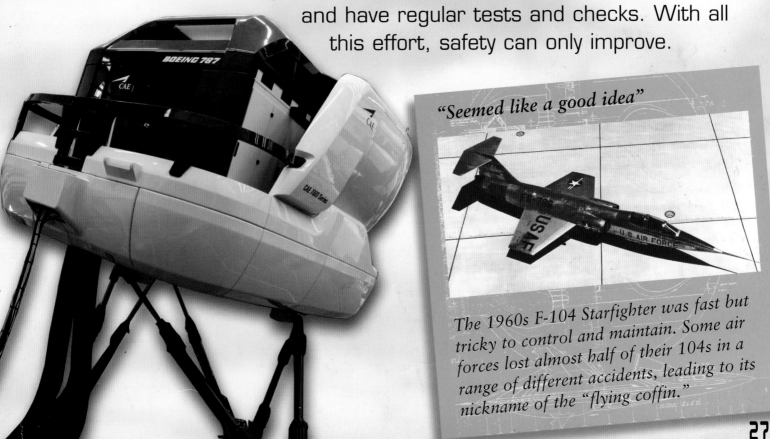

"Seemed like a good idea"

The 1960s F-104 Starfighter was fast but tricky to control and maintain. Some air forces lost almost half of their 104s in a range of different accidents, leading to its nickname of the "flying coffin."

U.S. AIR FORCE

FUTURE AIRPORTS

Aircraft of the future will be faster, safer, comfortable, and less harmful to the environment. What about airports? As air transport grows, they will have to cope with more people and cargo, faster and safer.

LESS WAITING TIME

Ticket, travel documents, passport, security, baggage check, body search ... airport passengers are soon worn out. Next-generation check-ins may be based on biometrics. These are detailed body measurements, from the eye's iris and retina to facial proportions, fingerprints, and voice analysis. Simply smile at the multi-cameras, say "Hi!," and you are identified as you.

In giant airports, planes are far from terminals. In the vertically integrated design (right) people park in the basement, check in just above, and take the escalator to the plane on top.

Airports often win awards for futuristic design, such as Incheon in South Korea.

"Seemed like a good idea...

In 1919, as air travel grew fast, planners imagined a raised rooftop airport in each city center. Like a raceway bowl, planes reached take-off speed by going round and round.

The Airborne Metro is a major interchange in the sky. As small cruisers come and go, passengers will change flights, just as we change trains when riding the subway.

MIT Double Bubble

The "Double Bubble" for 2035 has two fuselages joined along their length. Very light, and providing extra lift, the design could cut fuel use by two-thirds. Extra passenger doors allow faster loading and unloading at airports.

Three side-by-side turbofan engines

Extra doors

Future security scanners may work in "real time" so people are checked as they walk past, rather than waiting in lines. They will also see hidden weapons under clothing.

LOOK FURTHER!

This book is full of amazing ideas about air transport. What about even further ahead—the future of the future? Antigravity drives, space planes that hop around the world in a few hours ... who knows?

This NASA design for a 2,000 mph (3,200 km/h) airliner would cruise at the edge of space.

The WB1010 (below), part aircraft and part airship, carries 1,500 people at 650 mph (1,000 km/h). It might be in the sky by 2094.

The force of gravity pulls objects toward each other. Antigravity waves could cancel it out, allowing almost anything to fly.

Glossary

BWB, Blended Wing Body
A design that blends or merges the fuselage (main aircraft body) into the wing shape. It is often called the "flying wing."

Composites
Materials made from several substances like plastics, carbon or glass fibers, resins, and ceramics.

Contra-Rotating
Two sets of propellers or rotors on the same shaft that spin in opposite directions. Their blade angles are opposite, too, so they produce thrust in the same direction.

Drag
Air resistance—the force that slows any object trying to push past the tiny atoms and molecules of air.

Ducted Fan
A set of rotor blades like small propellers, called the fan, inside a collar or shroud shape, the duct.

Hybrid
A vehicle or craft with two forms of propulsion, such as a gasoline engine and an electric motor.

Lift
The force that pushes an aircraft up. It usually comes from the "aerofoil" shape of the wings, with a more curved upper surface than lower.

Solar Cells and Panels
Button-sized electronic devices that turn light into electrical energy. Many solar cells in one large sheet are a solar panel (solar array).

Supersonic
Faster than the speed of sound, which is usually 660 mph (1,062 km/h) at 20,000 feet (6,000 m).

Tailplane
Two small horizontal wings at the rear of most aircraft.

Thrust
The force that makes an aircraft move forward, from its propellers or from a jet or rocket engine.

Turbine
A rotating shaft with angled fan-shaped blades or rotors, which spin around when gases or liquids flow past them, or which turn to move a gas or liquid past them.

Index